Wonderful God

For Annie

Wonderful God

Text © Clare Horan 2009
Illustrations © Marcelle Krndija 2009

Photography / imaging by Matt Richards

ISBN 978 1 921472 12 1

Printed in China by Everbest

Published by
St Pauls Publications
P O Box 906, Strathfield NSW 2135, Australia

Wonderful God

By Clare Horan
Illustrations by Marcelle Krndija

ST PAULS

God creator, healer, friend,
God whose love will never end.
Wonderful God!
We see your love in mountain peaks,
in forests, deserts, flowing creeks,

in tiny flowers and shady trees,
in dewdrops and in mighty seas.
Wonderful God!

Your love gives life in falling rain,
in seeds that grow to fruit and grain,

in sun that shines and winds that blow,
and earth that nurtures plants to grow.
Wonderful God!

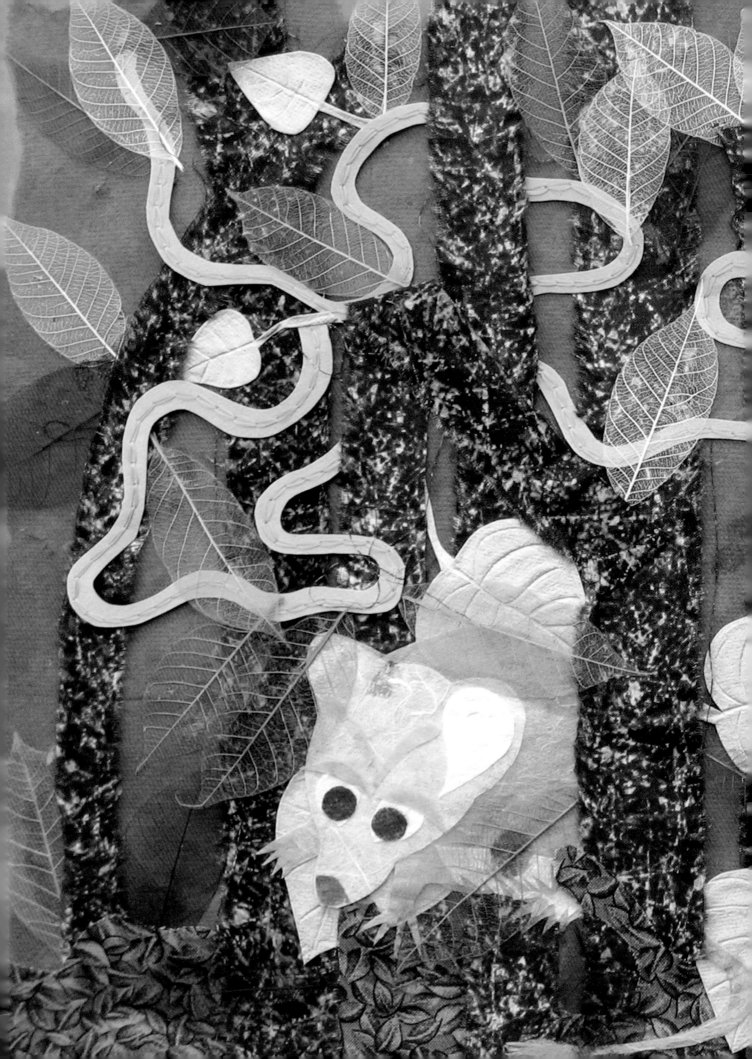

Your love's expressed in all your creatures,
each with its own special features,

called to be what it can be,
in space and air and land and sea.
Wonderful God!

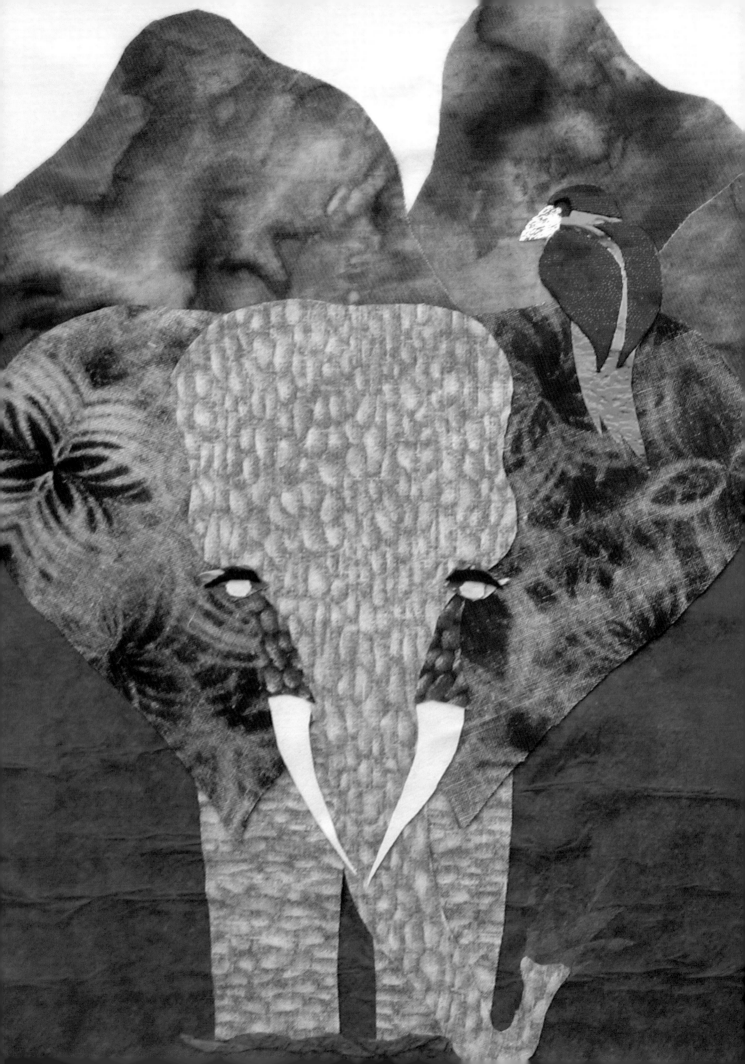

Marsupials, mammals,
fish and birds
that speak in whistles,
grunts and words:

you made us all to share one life.
If one is lost, we're all in strife.

Wonderful
God!

You're with us when we're hurt or sad.
You're near when times are good or bad.

You feel with us our joys and tears.
You understand mistakes and fears.
Wonderful God!

Your healing love brings brand new starts
to broken dreams and broken hearts,
to plans for good things gone astray,
to friendships that have lost their way.

Wonderful God!

You know our needs, you hear our prayers.
We're always in your loving care.

At home, at play, at work, at rest,
with your good gifts our lives are blest.
Wonderful God!

Your faithful love holds life in being.
In all that is, your love is freeing.

You give us freedom so we might choose to love and do what is right. Wonderful God!

You sent your love into our earth,
a human life that came to birth
in Bethlehem, without big fuss.
Jesus came: God-with-us.

Wonderful God!

He brought hope to sick and poor,
to sad and outcast, and what's more,

made compassion and forgiving,
love and peace the way for living.
Wonderful God!

but by justice, love and prayer,
kindness, open hearts and care.
Wonderful God!

We know from Jesus you're our friend.
We know your love will never end.

You are God of total grace.
Your love fills our every space.
Wonderful God!

God creator, healer, friend,
God, whose love will never end.
Wonderful God!